Write the Book You're Meant to Write

A Guide for First-time Authors

Write
the Book You're Meant to
Write

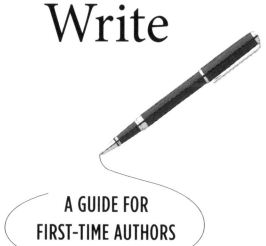

**A GUIDE FOR
FIRST-TIME AUTHORS**

GAIL WOODARD

DUDLEY COURT PRESS
Sonoita, Arizona

Published by:
Dudley Court Press, LLC
PO Box 102
Sonoita, AZ 85637
www.Dudley Court Press.com

Cover Design: Dunn+Associates
Interior Design: M. Urgo
Editor: Barbara McNichol

Paperback ISBN: 978-1-940013-37-4
Kindle ISBN: 978-1-940013-39-8
EPub ISBN: 978-1-940013-38-1

LCCN: 2017907535

Names: Woodard, M. Gail, author.
Title: Write the book you're meant to write : a guide for first-time authors / Gail Woodard.
Description: Sonoita, Arizona : Dudley Court Press, [2017] | Includes index.
Identifiers: ISBN: 978-1-940013-37-4 (paperback) | 978-1-940013-39-8 (Kindle) |
                978-1-940013-38-1 (ePub) | LCCN: 2017907535
Subjects: LCSH: Authorship. | Publishers and publishing. | Book industries and trade. | Manuscript
              preparation (Authorship) | Manuscript design. | Book design. | Booksellers and bookselling. |
              Books--Marketing. | Selling--Books. | BISAC: LANGUAGE ARTS & DISCIPLINES /
              Authorship. | LANGUAGE ARTS & DISCIPLINES / Publishing. | REFERENCE / Writing Skills.
Classification: LCC: PN187 .W66 2017 | DDC: 808.02--dc23

Connect with Gail Woodard at www.DudleyCourtPress.com

Join the DCP Book Reviewer Panel today. www.DudleyCourtPress.com/Reviewer-Panel.

Dedication

To Bob, who puts up with my crazy ideas,
listens to whatever I have to say,
and loves me with all my faults.

Contents

Preface

In 2008, I was bit by the "write a book" bug. In my case, the subject was my philosophy about living a joyful life. This passion turned into *Pay Attention, Say Thank You: Seven Rules for Joyful Living*.

I was a not a professional writer, though I had written plenty of corporate materials during my career as a strategic planner and marketer. I had also published articles as a free-lance travel writer. *Pay Attention, Say Thank You* emerged as one of those ideas that had to be written. Fortunately, I had the time and energy to write it at that point (plus a husband who brought me breakfast in bed most writing mornings. Every writer should be so lucky!)

About halfway through writing that book, I started to investigate possible publishing outlets. I admit it! I went through the phase of believing that everybody would/should read my book, that Oprah (still doing her TV show then) would LOVE my book, and that a New York publisher would be extremely lucky to get me to sign a contract… for a substantial advance, of course.

It took only two hours of Internet research for me to realize how far off base those fantasies were.

You see, I had no audience, no email list, no followers on Facebook or elsewhere in social media, and no platform for speaking. I was a nobody. And that meant my book would be very, very hard to sell to a publisher.

So I shifted gears and investigated the emerging world of self-publishing. I read the major books of the era, followed the new self-publishing gurus, and signed up with big self-publishing online services. Eventually, I figured out that these online "self-publishing" publishers were big-time marketing machines. They are in business to sell self-publishing services to anyone willing to give them a credit card number. They cared not a whit if my book had an audience nor about its quality. *True publishing partners work with authors to ensure a book is the best it can be, with a clear purpose and market.* But these publishing services companies are, in effect, marketing factories designed to separate authors from their money. They encourage hopeful but unwitting authors to purchase unneeded products and services—from poorly conceived cover designs and interior layouts to ineffective press releases—and deliver them in generic, templated formats.

Unlike true publishing partners who work with authors to ensure a book has a clear purpose and market, most publishing services companies are marketing factories that simply separate authors from their money.

As an experienced marketer, I could see the lack of value in their offerings. And shaking their sales people was tough. Once they had my email address and phone number, they dug in like pit bulls to sell, sell, sell. The calls from one company stopped only when I said the person they wanted to reach (me) had died!

This awful experience led me to start my own publishing company with the rights to publish my book. Because I wanted my book to look like it came from a traditional publisher, I invested in professional design, strong editing, and my own education about the publishing industry.

In 2009, *Pay Attention, Say Thank You* won a first-place Arizona Book Award for Religion/Spirituality. It has been published in a hardcover gift edition by New York publisher MJ Fine Books for sale in Barnes & Noble; it has also been published by Jaico Books for sale throughout the Indian sub-continent; and it has been translated into German for sale in Germany by a German publisher. My publishing company, Dudley Court Press, arranged the sales of all those rights, and I earned substantial royalty checks.

During the first few years of Dudley Court Press's existence, I published a half-dozen or more books for friends while learning about the industry and its fascinating changes. I've discovered I enjoy the business immensely—as much or more than I'd ever enjoyed working in banking or real estate during my early career. My team knows how to publish hardcover books, paperbacks, audio books, and e-books. In fact, two of our books were included in Apple's first iBooks catalog.

In addition to attending educational events in person and online, I've been to the big industry book fairs such as BEA (Book Expo America) and the London Book Fair. I have submerged myself in this tumultuous industry to figure out the pathways that make sense for the authors Dudley Court Press can assist.

In particular, I love the people in the industry, and I thoroughly enjoy the challenges that come with all the exciting changes. And what I've learned is simple: It's easy to publish a bad book and anyone can do it practically for free—except for the blood, sweat, and tears.

The blood and sweat, of course, refer to the time and effort it takes, and the tears come when the self-published author realizes all the mistakes and oversights. In book publishing, it's easy to do most everything wrong and look like an amateur. It's also easy to waste time and money doing what doesn't get you where you want to be.

In book publishing, it's easy to do most everything wrong and look like an amateur. It's also easy to waste time and money that doesn't get you where you want to be.

Yet it *is* possible to learn to publish well. I'm a walking example of that route. However, I'm a perfectionist. And when I dig into something, I become an expert. That's my nature.

Unfortunately most of the thousands of people who self-publish their books each month aren't able to develop the necesary background, education, or resources to effectively publish their own material. Their books are generally poorly conceived, poorly edited, poorly designed, and poorly marketed. They have NOT spent the megahours it takes to become educated about the industry and its nuances. Nor have they spent the money to bring expert editors and designers into the process of creating a great book. They don't understand the realities of the marketplace today. And generally, they end up disappointed with the results they achieve.

Sadly, most self-published authors never sell more than one or two hundred books. And they don't understand why. So my best advice is this:

- know your *real* reasons for writing your book,
- be clear about the market your book will thrive in,
- understand the true costs in time, energy, and money, and
- invest wisely in creating your book so your *real* goals can be met.

I sincerely hope this book helps you follow that advice. And click this link https:/www.DudleyCourtPress.com/GetStarted2 if you'd like to chat with me about *your* book. Best wishes!

Gail Woodard
Sonoita, AZ
August, 2017

Introduction

"You need to write a book!"

Have you heard that exhortation from acquaintances? Your business coach? Your family? Someone online? The media? That little voice inside your head?

In my role as publisher at Dudley Court Press, I speak with people all the time about their book ideas and dreams. Many sense they have a book inside them but aren't sure how to get started, or they've already worked hard to produce a manuscript but lack confidence about what to do next.

It's human nature to be timid about the unknown. For most people, writing and publishing a book is definitely unknown territory. Are you someone who gets stymied by the writing part? Or have you made it through the writing but feel overwhelmed by the publishing aspects?

I wrote this book because I want to dispel your fears, build your confidence, and make the unknown known to you.

It's a great time to be an author.

With the abundance of research, writing, and editing tools, digital publishing technologies plus social media and other marketing resources, authors have more opportunity today than ever to reach their desired audiences with better books. Of course, with all this technology, it's also easier to create poorly written, badly edited, or cheaply produced books. If you want to be taken seriously as an author and have your book reflect well on you as, say, an expert in your field, then publish your book professionally.

The good news is that you *can* educate yourself properly. You can learn what makes for a good book as well as understand publishing standards and economics. You can also find the right professional partners to help you. The more you know early in the process, the easier it will be to surmount the challenges and make informed, wise decisions.

The more you know early in the process, the easier it will be to surmount the challenges and make informed, wise decisions.

Yes, many decisions have to be made along the way. *Write the Book You're Meant to Write* can help you on your path to becoming an exceptional author—the most successful one you can be—as you produce a book you can be proud of.

Who will benefit from this book?

Whether you're writing fiction, nonfiction, or memoir, this book is for you. Whether your book idea has kept you company for years or it's a recent thought of intrigue, keep reading. If the *idea* of writing a book feels like a possibility you want to know more about, you're reading the right book. And it's for you if your goal is any of the following:

- Fulfill a promise to yourself.
- Generate leads for your business.

- Boost your credibility or celebrity status in your field.
- Share your ideas and wisdom with others.
- Entertain readers with your wit or imagination.
- Showcase accomplishments—yours and/or others'.
- Help those who share your challenge by telling your story.
- Provide instruction or education in your area of expertise.
- Leave a legacy for your family.
- Encapsulate your experiences so others can benefit from them.
- Meet a challenge from your business or writing coach.
- Better understand your own situation or experience.
- Fulfill a big dream you've entertained for a long time.

What's in *Write the Book You're Meant to Write?*

This book has been structured purposefully. *Part One* helps you figure out if you're ready to write, or if it's better to move on to something else. The result? You'll be able to clarify *what* you intend to write and feel confident you are writing the *right* book for you.

In these first three chapters, you'll find many of the questions we work through with clients during our Strategy Sessions at Dudley Court Press. By answering the questions deliberately, you'll develop the confidence and self-assurance needed to move forward.

The next three chapters, *Part Two*, address important fundamentals to become clear about as you embark on your journey as an author. It debunks common myths about publishing and offers insights into practical considerations for writers of fiction, nonfiction, and memoir. It also clarifies the distinctions among various types of publishing approaches.

Part Three provides an overview of the publishing journey and covers metadata, distribution, and marketing. It features Q & A sessions with three industry professionals: an award-winning book cover designer, a book designer with decades of experience, and an editor with more than 340 edited books to her credit. They offer insights into the key elements for success for any author as they answer this question: *What does a first-time author need to know?*

The *Conclusion* nudges you on your way, helping you take the next steps to writing the book you're meant to write.

Do you want to write a book that has commercial potential, or do you intend to produce one strictly for personal use? Either is fine; each direction suggests certain choices.

Exploring various avenues for your book, understanding what's possible, and making conscious choices from the beginning can save you time, energy, money, and frustration down the road.

I wish you a grand journey of success as you become an exceptional author. Write and publish a meaningful book. Do it right. Do it well. And enjoy every step along the way.

Part One

Preparation

Chapter 1

The Call to Write a Book

Is this you?

You've been writing stories or working on a novel on the side, perfecting your craft, perhaps for years. Or you're a thoughtful, engaged person busy with your career or on the cusp of a new role as a business, community, or family elder. Whether you think of yourself as a writer or not, *the idea of writing a book keeps recurring as something you need to do.* Do you see yourself in these scenarios?

- Like me, you may have a few gray hairs that go along with your experience, accomplishments, and wisdom about your life, your profession, and your avocations. You may be pondering the legacy you'll leave behind. *And a book seems to be the answer.*

- Or you may be like me a decade ago, looking for a way to share your knowledge, help others, strengthen your professional stature, or enjoy the creative process. *And a book seems to be the answer.*

- You may have written fiction, poetry, essays or short stories for along time and finally, you know *it's time to get your work published—as a book.*

- You may be approaching or well into your retirement years—though for you, retirement means a shift to a new career or passion, not the end of living a meaningful life. You care about your emerging role as a family, business, or community elder, a wise one, a mentor. *And a book seems to be the answer.*

- Or perhaps you repeatedly hear from your business coach or experts at business development seminars that you need a book. You're told, "A book is the new business card" and "everyone needs a lead generation book today." *A book seems to be the answer.*

If this is you…you're in good company.

Whether you're writing non-fiction to enhance your professional stature, fiction to entertain, or memoir to share stories with your family, you're in good company. Imagine! Eighty-six percent of Americans say they want to write a book! Thousands of baby boomers and pre-boomers *are* writing books today. Given the widespread availability of publishing technology, it's become a popular undertaking—as evidenced by Amazon listing more than 200,000 new titles every single month!

Books, of course, range in quality from exceptional to, let's say, unfortunate.

Books range in quality from exceptional to, let's say, unfortunate.

If quality matters to you, you'll find aligned guidance in this book. Its purpose is to help you *consciously choose to become an exceptional author of a quality book* published in a professional manner. You can be deemed *exceptional* even if you write only one small book with *quality built into its content and production.*

Whether as a collection of family stories or compendium of wisdom, our life lessons *want* to be transmitted to others. Oldsters of all types want to share their life stories with family. Late career and retired professionals feel a strong desire to share their knowledge, wisdom, and passions through a book. Entrepreneurs want to educate their potential clients and inspire confidence in their services.

Most of these folks don't call themselves authors, but they realize the book format is their preferred outlet.

The call to write a book may come as a business decision.

Many professionals realize a book can help them leverage their credibility and expert status, thus aiding in their business development as a high-class business card. These examples reflect a variety of purposes:

- One professional wrote his book to help explain his niched but complex financing projects related to building medical facilities in rural areas. His book—an authoritative-looking hardcover—supplemented his presentations to corporate boards and enhanced his status with potential clients.

"My Ideas are Full-time"

Here's what Martha Johnson, former administrator of the U.S. General Services Administration under President Obama, said about why she wanted to write her book: "I am not a full-time writer but my ideas are full time, and a book is one way to get them transferred to other people."

Martha Johnson, On My Watch: Leadership, Innovation and Personal Resilience. *Published by Dudley Court Press, 2012 [http://bit.ly/OnMyWatch-DCP]*

- Another wrote a book about management issues in the government contracting industry. After he retired from his long, distinguished career, his book became a textbook in the graduate business program where he'd become a visiting instructor.

- A career coach wrote a book to delineate her process and leveraged it into landing media appearances and larger contracts.

- An osteopathic physician wrote a book about alternative, holistic treatments for drug users. He listed it as the first asset in a new business model for his medical practice, which included speaking engagements and training other professionals.

- An online marketing professional's book helped elevate him to guru status within his industry.

The call to write a book may reflect a personal purpose.

- One 78-year-old man started his memoir because he figured he wouldn't be around when his grandchildren were old enough to appreciate his stories. They included helping build the Arizona Trail, taking deep-sea diving trips in Costa Rica, and living in Ecuador for four years—an adventure he'd just completed. He wanted to capture his adventures in writing because, as he told me, "I just want my kids and grandkids to know I had a good life."

- Another man wanted to tell the story of his famous football-player father, who inspired the crew of a World War II bomber.

- A woman who had extricated herself from a viciously abusive family wanted to tell her story to break the bonds that had institutionalized abuse throughout generations of her extended family.

- Four women who had endured well-meaning but painful comments after their children had died dreamed of writing a book to express better ways to support a grieving mother.

The call to write a book comes from well-meaning friends.

Many people tell me their friends and family are always saying, "You should write a book!" Have you heard that, too?

Perhaps because you're a great storyteller or have experiences no one else has. Or perhaps they know how much effort you have put into your fiction-writing and they want you to be recognized as a published author.

You could ignore the call as before. But perhaps you're now wondering if you *should* listen.

Are you listening to the call?

For some people, the call comes clearly and they respond with confidence. For others, it's dismissed or ignored—for a while. Eventually, they listen, but with reluctance or resistance.

"Really? Me? Write a book?"

"Is that possible?"

"Could I ever do that?"

I suggest letting go of the resistance and seeing how far the call takes you. You don't have to commit to anything quite yet; just explore it for a bit.

Take ownership of the call. See how far you get.

---

*Let go of the resistance and see how far
the call takes you.*

Creative impulses such as the call to write a book come as opportunities to expand your experience of life. The more often you say "Yes!" the richer and more satisfying a life you can experience.

So, pay attention to the impulses calling you. Follow them until you have a clear sense of what it will feel like to write and finish your book and hold that printed book in your hands.

If the desire is strong enough, you'll find a way to move forward.

Reasons to write your book ... soon

Here are several reasons to answer the call sooner than later:

- You have overcome a tremendous challenge with grace and good humor, and you could be a role model for others. The sooner you write your book, the more people you can help.

- You have said "Yes!" to so much of what life offers that your story will inspire others—or at least entertain them. The sooner you write your book, the more people will benefit.

- You have acquired a wealth of wisdom, and publishing a book will allow you to share it broadly. The sooner you write it, the more people will benefit from your wisdom.

- You have quietly expressed yourself creatively through writing, and it's time to produce a product you can share with the world. The sooner you devote yourself to sharing your work, the richer your life will be.

- You want to share your life stories with your family before your time runs out. Age comes upon us when we're not looking, so sooner is better than not at all.

- You want to take your life in a new direction, and a book will help you establish credibility as an expert. And the sooner you get your book published, the sooner you'll achieve a higher status in your field.

- You're over 50 or 60 or 70 or 80 and your life energy will eventually wane. Far too many people wait until they can't write, or remember, anymore.

- You're under 50 and eager to break out of the crowd in your field. A book can establish you as an authority. And the sooner you write it, the sooner you will enjoy the leverage it can bring.

The sooner you write your book, the sooner you will enjoy the leverage it can bring.

To author a book is infinitely special. It takes commitment, a sense of purpose, and a good deal of time and energy to see it through from idea to finished product. Those who follow the call from wanting-to-write-a-book to being-a-published-author undertake a path that can be both exhilarating and hugely frustrating. And if you do things right, becoming a published author can be extraordinarily satisfying.

I encourage you to make your choice sooner than later.

What if you're not ready?

Sometimes the time just isn't right to dedicate yourself to writing a book. I get that. And there's nothing wrong with deciding NOT to write a book. In my work with authors over the years, I've learned that your WHY—the emotional payoff you attach to getting your book written—has to be strong enough or you won't succeed. In the next section, you'll explore the reasons you *want* to write your book. If your emotional payoff isn't enough, then not answering the call is perhaps the better decision.

Here's the key: *Be conscious about your choice.* Let me share my "unanswered calls" with you to show you what I mean.

My unanswered calls (i.e., the books I haven't yet written)

People have often encouraged me to write a book about homeschooling my three sons. During those years, we traveled a lot and lived in Mexico and France. I've barely managed to organize photos and journals of those years for the family. And I know that capturing those years is something I'll do—but only for family. The world will have to live without that book on Amazon.

I've got a half-written book about my year on Match. com, the dating site, after my divorce. It's called, cleverly, *My Year on Match.com.* I kept the book's URL, but it hasn't been touched in 10 years. I have too many other projects more interesting than this!

While living in France with my sons in 2000–2001, I was deeply drawn into the experiences of both *La Resistance* and the *les femmes tondues*—the shorn women—who were accused of collaboration with the Germans during World War II. (Their neighbors dragged these women from their homes, stripped them, shaved their heads and paraded them through the town. Sometimes these women were marked with swastikas, tarred or beaten to death.) One woman, Charlotte (real or imagined), entered my consciousness and wanted her story told. It would be set in the town of St. Martin-en-Haut in the hills around Lyon. My files still contain notes and books about the town, which I visited. But I have not yet felt up to this call. Frankly, this one terrifies me. It would challenge all my writing skills and, as historical fiction, demand more of me than any other book I've written or considered.

As you can see, I've made conscious choices about all three of these calls. None of the books are important enough to me—yet—to take my time from other activities. I do like knowing the projects are there, in boxes, in case I want to tackle them. However, if I never write those books, I won't have regrets because I've made conscious choices about them along the way.

Please do that for yourself. *Choose consciously* to move forward with your book idea, or *choose consciously* to put it on a shelf, or *choose consciously* to toss the whole idea in the trash.

Make the right decision for *you*. Without regret.

Chapter 2

Are You Ready to Write Your Book?

If you're not an experienced writer, you may wonder if you can get the job done. Most of our clients at Dudley Court Press are NOT primarily writers. We help them decide if they have the stamina, gumption, and foundation to successfully write and market their books. This chapter is designed to help YOU determine if YOU are ready to write your book.

How do you know if you've got what it takes?

When you feel that pull to share your story or knowledge through a book, how do you know if the pull is strong enough to see you through the entire journey? Here are three questions to ask. And there are no right or wrong answers. Know that *your* answers will help you understand where you are on the publishing path and how committed you are to your book project.

First: What is your WHY?

It's helpful to write your responses to these questions, especially if you're determined that *now* is the time to "fish or cut bait," as my dad used to say.

- WHY do you want to write a book now?
  - ► Do you sense that a book is the right tool to help you establish a new career at this stage of your life?
  - ► Do you want to share your wisdom or tell an important story while you still can?
  - ► Do you have another reason unique to you?

- Do you have the time, energy, and money to invest in a book project now? What resources do you think it will require?

- What impact do you hope your book will have?

- What's the payoff for you if you write and publish this book?

- Is this payoff sufficient for you to dedicate the time, energy, and money to make your book all you want it to be?

If your answer to this last question is "no," then stop here. Find another way to spend your time.

Your WHY contains the emotional reasons that will sustain you when the writing gets tough or the publishing process frustrates you or the marketing feels unending. Your WHY underlies your answer to the call.

Your WHY must be strong enough to keep you going through the challenges inherent in the process of writing and publishing a book.

If your WHY doesn't feel strong enough to carry you through the project, simply give yourself permission to let it go. Here's an example of a client who consciously changed direction.

> A woman felt she should write a book about a business software process for users for which she was an acknowledged expert. She knew a strong written resource for those users didn't exist. After gaining a clear picture of what was involved in writing, publishing, and marketing a book successfully, she decided it just wasn't right for her. She acknowledged she was tired of the corporate world and wanted a change, so she decided to follow a long-time dream of renovating houses.

Second: Do you feel a strong emotional attachment?

If your WHY is strong, continue to answer the following questions to beef up your motivation while strengthening your emotional attachment to getting the book done.

- What will it feel like to you to hold your book in your hands, finally? (Take time to imagine this feeling. You might even make a mock-up of a book with your title and name on the front. See what THAT does to your motivation!)

- What do you imagine your life will be like when you've completed your book?

- How will it be different from your life now?

- How will YOU be different?

Imagining the future you want is the first step to getting there, so take time to think about how a published book will affect you and your life. Will it take you to a place you want to be?

Of course, it's helpful to hold a realistic vision. From time to time, we have to explain that the dream of sitting-on-the-beach-drinking-Pina-Coladas-while the-publisher-sends-royalty-checks is fantasy, not vision.

Better to imagine yourself speaking to audiences about your story or cause. Maybe you'll do radio interviews or Skype sessions with library patrons and book clubs. Maybe you'll teach courses or workshops. (Of course, you could always organize a workshop near the beach….)

Whether your answer to the call to write a book is a strong "Yes!" or even "Maybe" or "I'm not sure," you'll want to know more about how to proceed to write, publish, and market a book in today's world. There's much to learn so you can confidently write the right book that fulfills your goals and supports your personal vision.

Third: Do you know your weaknesses and strengths?

Dig deeper to understand your weaknesses and strengths as they relate to writing your book. As you meet yourself honestly by answering these questions, you'll be clearing your own path. You'll learn more about your fears or beliefs, and you'll start to grasp the ways you can take action, if that's what you really want to do. So, again, take time to reflect and jot down your answers to these questions. Then consider what options you've identified to help you move forward.

- Why haven't you written and published your book yet? What's held you back?
    - ► Do you lack time or resources?
    - ► Do you fear the unknown?
    - ► Are you confused or overwhelmed at all the options today?
    - ► Do you feel insecure or anxious about doing it all wrong?
    - ► Haven't you found guidance you trust?

- Do you think you can write decently?
    - ► If you're not a good writer, are you willing and able to hire a ghostwriter or work intensively with a professional editor so your book meets editorial quality standards?

- Even if you (think you) are a good writer, are you willing to work with a professional editor to ensure your book meets editorial quality standards?

- What are your qualifications that permit you to write the book you envision?

- Do you have the time, energy, and determination to write a 20,000- to 80,000-word book at this time in your life?

- Do you know how long YOUR book should be to meet your goals and fit the market?

- Do you have the time, energy, and resources to market your book once it's published?

- Do you have a defined, established audience for your book?

Knowing what you *don't* know is a common challenge for first-time authors. So often, they don't think about who will buy and read their book until after they've finished their manuscripts. It's natural but unfortunate, for much time and money can be saved by having the proper strategy in place early in the process.

Much time and money can be saved by having the proper strategy in place early in the process.

Here's a story about a client who illustrates the message in this chapter and the next. It points out the importance of knowing the *right* book to write.

One Veterinarian's Dream

One client came to us with a desire to write a book of stories (in the tradition of James Herriot) about the pets she'd cared for as a veterinarian. During our Strategy Session, it became clear she had an even stronger desire to spread her message of death experiences that were peaceful for both pets and their owners.

As a result of our Strategy Session, she set aside the pet stories book for now to focus on her professional message of peaceful pet transitions. However, she wasn't ready to write that book because the process had only been used in her own practice.

She followed our recommendations to build her credibility and expert status by implementing a training program for veterinarians. In it, she teaches her methods and the eco-

nomic benefits of employing them for peaceful pet transitions. Over time, she has partnered with individuals and institutions to teach these methods, gain valuable feedback, and develop case studies.

As a result, her eventual book on this subject will be rich and authoritative because of the experience and data she's gathering beyond her own practice. Her book of pet stories, which she still intends to write, will then have a larger audience because she's building a base with her trainings. Her pet stories book will become another asset in her business.

Every Author Today = Writer + Marketer

By the way, many authors are dismayed to learn that *writing* a book is the easy part. To be a successful author today, you not only need to write your book but you need to *market* it deliberately and consistently. *This is true whether you're writing fiction or non-fiction and regardless of the the publishing route you take.*

So the question goes beyond "Am I ready to write my book?" You also need to ask, "Am I ready to market my book?" Chapter 10 begins an explanation of book marketing. However, the best initial marketing is built into your book—its title, subtitle, cover design, description, category selection, and other metadata elements.

Your first and best marketing starts now—and never ends. Getting professional guidance is a wise step!

Chapter 3

What's the Right Book to Write?

Millions of new books are published every year, yet most never sell more than 100 copies.

Certainly, many people write books they never intend to sell in the commercial marketplace. In fact, at Dudley Court Press, in addition to publishing commercial fiction and nonfiction books, we frequently publish memoirs strictly for private use. We enjoy helping those clients produce books they can proudly deliver to friends and family.

However, many authors unwittingly write and publish books that have no promise of any acceptance in any marketplace at all. *Don't be one of them.*

Many authors unwittingly write and publish books with no promise of acceptance in any marketplace. Don't be one of them!

How can you know?

Let's start by pointing out characteristics of what we might call "unexceptional" authors. They are people who:

- Fail to educate themselves sufficiently before diving in.
- Think "everyone" will love their book or "should" read it.
- Assume that because they know how to read a book, they also know how to write and publish one!
- Do little market research to identify and find likely readers.
- Have limited understanding of the economics of publishing.

Online as well as in-person study groups are well populated with aspiring but usually disappointed, frustrated, and often whiny authors. But if you're reading *this* book, chances are you aren't one of those whiny authors. *Smart authors realize that navigating the complex world of publishing today can be daunting. They opt for professional guidance.*

What are your goals?

At Dudley Court Press, we start by assessing the viability of the book concept in terms of the author's self-proclaimed goals. We help our clients understand how their books fit into a broader picture. An example is the veterinarian noted in the previous chapter.

Here's another example of how we help our clients figure out the right book to write.

Memoir to Fact-Based Book to Memoir

When Paul Golden, M.D., first came to Dudley Court Press, he'd spent the year after his retirement writing his memoir. Dur-

ing our Strategy Session, when probed about why he wanted to publish his memoir, he said that if someday someone found his memoir on a shelf at Barnes & Noble and it was helpful to that person, he would be happy. His comment opened the door to a broad discussion about his potential role as an advocate and speaker—a role he had never considered.

Ultimately, we helped Dr. Golden write a small, fact-based educational book titled An Insider's View of Bipolar Disease. *This established him as an authority and helped generate media interest and speaking engagements.*

A year after his first book was published, we published his memoir, Bipolar MD: My Life As a Physician with Bipolar Disorder. *By then, he had a ready audience and could bolster his appeal as a speaker, interview subject, and authority.*

The memoir alone would not have positioned him as an expert. But paired with his first book, it now serves him well. You can find out more about Dr. Golden at www.mdgolden. com.

What's your book about?

To answer this question, distill the central message of your book down to a 25-word blurb. This is one of the most challenging but *productive* exercises you can do as a writer. Having that short description is like having a target in front of you as you sit down to write each day.

To help you get clear about the target, review these questions:

- What do you want to write about?
    - ► Do you have a significant collection of wisdom and knowledge that you don't want to

see disappear with you and feel passionate to share?

- ► Or do you have a story to tell that celebrates the achievements of others you know well?
- ► Or do you believe that your own story, well told, will inspire or help others who face the challenges you have faced?

- Is your fiction topic of interest to a large enough audience?

- Can you summarize the topic of your book in 200 words in a way that will attract potential readers?

- Next, can you do that in 25 words?

- Do you have an outline of your book? (Craft a detailed Table of Contents to serve as a roadmap during the writing stage.)

- Who is the audience for your book?
    - ► Why will they want to read your book?
    - ► What value will it bring to them?

- Does your book provide information, inspiration, or entertainment?

- Is your book designed so your readers will understand its relevance to them right away? (If it's confusing, it's not meaningful.)

- What four or five books are similar to yours? How is yours different?

Sometimes, a book makes more economic or commercial sense if split into more than one volume. Other times, it will fare better in the marketplace written as fiction rather than nonfiction. Maybe the right book is just a sliver of the knowledge an author would like to share. Each circumstance depends on where he or she strives to be, and where the ideal book audience can be found.

Who is your book for?

Understand your reasons for writing and publishing your book early so you can make wise choices as you move along the publishing path. If you intend to use it to further your career or enhance your professional status, you must understand that the quality of your book—content and production—should be high. After all, this book represents *you* and your message to the world. On the other hand, if your book is primarily for your family and close friends, you have more leeway in terms of choices.

If your book is related to your professional status in any way, get clear on how you'll use it and with whom so it effectively serves your career. For example, if you intend to use your book to establish your professional credibility with executives in boardroom settings, your book likely should be produced as a hardcover. It may be a good idea for the cover to include an impressive photo of you as well.

If your book is related to your professional status in any way, get clear on how you'll use it and with whom so it effectively serves your career.

By comparison, if your audience is high school students or people with low reading levels, a thin paperback with lots of illustrations or cartoons will help you reach your audience more effectively than a dense, 300-page book.

Not only do we see clients whose initial book ideas fail to serve their broader goals, but we also encounter book projects that, as presented, don't make economic sense. In some cases, we think it would work better as fiction rather than nonfiction. Helping our clients determine the best book for them to write is one of our first goals. Make sure the book *you* are writing will, indeed, fulfill your goals.

Are you considering the self-publishing route?

As mentioned earlier, I believe we're fortunate to live in an age when writers can finally hold in their hands a properly bound edition of the book they've spent so much effort to create without working with a traditional publisher. It's a satisfying feeling.

But remember this: Don't confuse the *availability of the technology* to create a complete, bound book with any assurance of market viability. Not every person who auditions for America's Got Talent makes an appearance on the live show.

If you simply want to get your book designed and encased with a cover, you can do that quickly and easily through many of the online publishing vendors or even at a local print shop. Do be aware that your book will be well received only by your family and friends who love you. It's unlikely to find an audience beyond your close circle, no matter how much you think *everybody* will love it or needs it. (Please read this blog post before you go too far with the big online "self-publishing" companies so you don't get caught in their traps: https://www.dudleycourtpress.com/author-solutions-be-warned)

Is your book idea viable?

If you are wondering if your book idea is the *right* book for *you* to write, please talk with a professional—book coach, a literary agent, a developmental editor, someone—*before* you go further with your project. Whether you are writing fiction or nonfiction, strategic planning and a clear understanding of how your book fits your overall goals is important to your book's eventual success.

Part Two

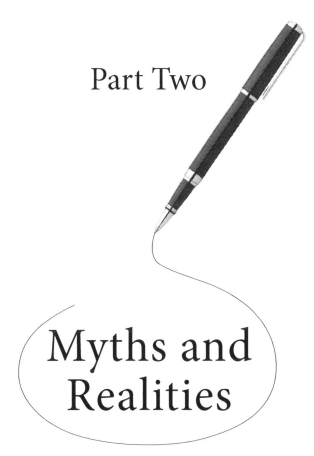

Myths and Realities

Chapter 4

Four Myths about Publishing Busted

Over the past two decades, the once staid and predictable publishing industry has been turned inside out. It has re-emerged with a gazillion new players, new relationships, new technologies, and new delivery systems. All the change has created confusion, wasted wanderings down the wrong paths, and plain old overwhelm for everyone in the industry, newcomer or old guard.

This volatility can create great opportunities for exceptional authors like you—*as long as you don't fall victim to major misconceptions and sales pitches prevalent today.*

Here are four myths about book publishing to examine:

Myth #1: It's easy to publish and sell a high-quality book today.

Myth #2: Anyone can publish a quality book at no or low cost.

Myth #3: A book is a fast, sure road to riches.

Myth #4: Writing the book is the hard part.

Myth #1: It's easy to publish and sell a high-quality book today.

While you'll often hear "it's easy for anyone to publish a book today," what you don't hear is how challenging it is to both *publish* and *sell* a professional-quality book. Wonderful technologies and online publishing resources make it seem so simple to print books that kindergarteners could do it. If you want to publish a book for family and friends, you can. No problem.

However, if you're writing your book to share broadly with the world and/or you intend to sell your book, it's critical to recognize that the amateur approach is *not* your best option.

Think of it this way:

- Just because you can apply paint to canvas doesn't mean your finished product belongs in the Louvre.

- Just because you can sing and dance a bit doesn't mean you are ready to appear in Broadway shows.

- Just because you put 40,000 words together in a Word document doesn't mean your book is ready for the marketplace or is destined for the best-seller lists.

If you're writing your book to share broadly with the world and/or you intend to sell your book, it's critical to recognize that the amateur approach is not your best option

---

Imagine if there were an Author/Book Edition of *America's Got Talent.* How many of the thousands of authors would make it through the auditions to the Top Ten?

That was a trick question. But I hope you see my point.

Millions of new books are published every year and most never sell more than 100 copies. It's NOT easy to publish a high-quality book.

Did you know Amazon alone adds nearly 200,000 new titles EVERY SINGLE MONTH? How would anyone find YOUR book?

Yes, there are ways to improve your chances of success, of course, and this book offers suggestions to help you get closer to a spot on the live show, so to speak. But don't ever fall for the myth that the path is an easy one.

To publish a professional-quality book—

- takes extreme attention to detail,

- requires high standards for the editorial and design elements,

- involves a broad understanding of industry requirements, and

- demands an appreciation of the entire design, printing, distribution, and marketing aspects of book publishing today.

If you don't want your book to look amateurish, get professional help—now!

Myth #2: Anyone can publish a quality book at no or low cost.

Do you want to publish a book you can be proud of—one that reflects your professional stature and can hold its own next to traditionally published books from New York publishers? Well, that doesn't come free.

To publish a successful, meaningful book, you need—

- professional editing so the book reads well and will generate positive reviews.

- professional design work for the cover and the interior.

- marketing strategies and the ability to implement them.

- certainty of the size and presentation of the book (i.e., does it conform to what your audience expects?).

- knowledge of using metadata.

- placement of your book into databases and distribution and sales channels (unless you intend to sell only from the trunk of your car).

All of these require resources—time, talent, knowledge—that cost money to acquire. And as with most things, you get what you pay for. Spending a lot does not guarantee you'll have a best-seller. But ignoring key requirements in book production and discoverability factors, for example, will guarantee low or no sales.

Exceptional authors understand this. They do the research necessary to find the right partners who will help them do these activities well.

Myth #3: A book is a fast, sure road to riches.

Let's bust that myth quickly.

Even among well-established writers, advances from their traditional publishers have dropped significantly in recent years. For well-known authors, advances that used to be in the $50,000 to $100,000 range are much lower today. Sometimes the advances from traditional publishers are as low as $5,000—and that's for established authors!

To add to that, few new authors are brought into traditional publishing houses under old-fashioned contracts. What do the major publishing houses want? They contract for blockbuster titles from popular authors such as John Grisham, Nora Roberts, David Baldacci and celebrities.

Even to be considered by a traditional publisher, authors must demonstrate that they have a vast, solid audience already in place. If you don't have that, you'll waste your time looking for a traditional publisher.

Some people hype the data showing that more than 1,000 indie authors are making at least $50,000 a year in book earnings on Amazon alone! What they don't point out is that with more than two million new titles added each year, *the percentage of authors who make much money is miniscule.*

Very few authors enjoy a direct financial return on their investment in writing and publishing a book.

Authorearnings.com scrapes data from Amazon to provide reports about author earnings from book sales on Amazon. While their numbers don't include non-Amazon book sales, it's among the best data available to approximate author earnings.

Let's assume all authors contribute two new titles a year, so the number of authors represented would be 1.2 million. That means that less than one-tenth of one percent of authors are making $50,000 or more from their Amazon sales. And that isn't a lot, folks!

Very few authors enjoy a direct financial return on their investment in writing and publishing a book.

To recoup your investment in a book, you and your publisher depend on the profits from book sales. The profit margin on a book depends on various decisions about manufacturing and distribution. And pricing is quite sensitive to the marketplace.

There are ways to cover costs and, for many authors, their return on investment goes beyond book sales or royalties. Speaking and consulting fees often go up with the publication of a book—when it's done professionally. And fiction authors MUST understand the need for multiple titles, Write book two before your release book one!

Myth #4: Writing the book is the hard part.

While they're tearing their hair out to get the manuscript into shape, it's difficult to tell authors that typing "The End" marks the beginning, not the end. Writing your book can be hard, of course. But once it's done, the writing is deemed the easy part.

It's the marketing of your book that's especially hard. And it never stops.

As I've mentioned, over two million books are added to Amazon's inventory of print, e-book, and audio books every year. Without intentional and strategic work during its development and production stages, your book will languish as one of those unknown, unfound, and unsold products on Amazon.

So when you embark on your publishing journey, get good advice about the necessary fundamentals to establish your marketing platform and develop a good marketing plan. Publishing your book so the metadata can clearly support your marketing efforts is crucial.

If your metadata is incomplete or wrong,
your book will never show up when someone
(or a search engine robot) searches for your
title or subject.

Metadata is the information used by the publishing industry to identify and categorize your book in a myriad of systems. These include sales, marketing, and data systems at Amazon and other retailers, libraries, Bowker's Books-in-Print, Google Books, and search engines, among others. If your metadata is incomplete or wrong, your book will never show up when someone (or a search engine robot) searches for your title or subject.

Working with a trusted publisher helps ensure that your book:

- meets commercial industry standards,
- has a strong title to help readers discover it,
- sports a cover that markets your book effectively,

- has a design that's aligned to your genre and audience,
- is categorized properly to ensure it can be found electronically,
- includes descriptions in the right places to help with discoverability.

It's extremely easy to mess up these details. The most common examples include bad book titles and poor cover designs. These elements are critical to your book being discovered. Here's why:

- Obscure titles don't sell books.
- Book covers that confuse readers are useless.
- So are those that can't be discerned or read at postage-stamp size.

Having your own or your publisher's experience with these kinds of issues helps overcome the challenges of SELLING your book.

Chapter 5

Are You Writing Fiction, Nonfiction, or Memoir?

This chapter digs deeper into the writing process itself and practical considerations that go into wise book publishing today.

Are you writing fiction or nonfiction or memoir?

First, let's talk about the *type* of book you will write.

For most people, it's clear whether they're writing ***fiction*** (a novel, novella, collection of short stories, all fabricated) or ***nonfiction*** (fact-based, instructional, informational, truth-telling). ***Historical fiction*** crosses over because it uses documented events, places, and people crafted into a made-up story line.

Memoir is a nonfiction category, but the best of literary memoirs incorporate the important writing elements of fiction such as plot and character development.

Writing the truth as fiction

Sometimes an author chooses to write as fiction something that's essentially true—which is entirely acceptable. In fact, for some writers, this proves to be a formidable strategy.

Have you encountered authors whose personal stories were so dramatic or extraordinary that they *should* be written as fiction rather than nonfiction/memoir? The lives of these authors who wanted to write multiple books gave them exciting material to work with. Audiences would be happy to read a series of princess-to-spiritual-guru-to-farmer books or double-agent-spy books with strong plots and captivating characters. Indeed, they'd be bored or irritated reading page after page of "me, me, me," which is what the books would become if written as memoir.

Sometimes an author chooses to write as fiction something that's essentially true—which is entirely acceptable.

This approach is smart if you want to write multiple books and have exceptional life experiences to work from. As any writer of fiction, though, you'll need to hone your story-writing and plot-crafting skills.

Writing non-truths as truth

The reverse is not acceptable—that is, passing off something as true or nonfiction when it's contrived. Memoirs are tricky in this regard. You may recall highly publicized scandals involving celebrity memoirs that were essentially fabrications.

One author, James Frey, was famously held accountable by Oprah Winfrey in a live, face-to-face confrontation on her television show after the veracity of his book, which had been selected by Oprah for her book club, had been questioned.

Know the line between fabrication and details you actually remember.

Fiction writing is a skill, an art, and a business.

If you are writing fiction, be sure your writing skills are strong. Here are four ideas to help you improve your writing abilities:

Take writing classes. You can find classes in your local area at community colleges and adult education programs, or look online. When I searched for "writing classes online" Google returned 144 million results. I'll be you can find a course and venue that works for you.

Join a writing group. Ask around. You're likely to find a writer's group you can join. Or start one of your own. You can even find a group of people in far-flung locations, share your work by email and enjoy Skype conversations together.

Participate in NaNo WriMo (National Novel Writing Month). NaNo WriMo is a free online community writing event every November that attracts hundreds of thousands of participants from all over the world. You start writing on November 1st and stop on November 30th at midnight. If you complete 50,000 words, you're a winner. Use NaNoWriMo as a way to quicken your writing pace, dive deep into your book to get it done and enjoy camaraderie with other writers. Go to www.nanowrimo.com

Learn to work with editors. Find local editors, or hire someone through Upwork.com or other freelancing website. Start small, with a few chapters or a short story. Invest in your own education about how best to work with an editor, what kind of editor you need, and how the author-editor relationship works. Your writing should improve as you work with an editor, and your appreciation for the complexities of getting a manuscript ready for publication will expand.

Consider your brand and your business

As an author of fiction, think in terms of your brand and your business. After all, you are creating product and your audience, if they like you, will be loyal and read everything you produce. Any reader who enjoys a book of fiction naturally looks for another book by that author.

For this reason, here is the most important advice I can give writers of fiction: *Have your second book ready before you release your first.* I know this sounds daunting if you're struggling to get the first book written, but here's the thing: in order to sell your book, you need to reach readers. That takes time, effort and money. If you have a second book available, readers will buy it and your investment in marketing brings you two sales rather than one. If you have only one book for readers to buy, and a long period of time (a year or more) passes before you release your second book, they'll forget about you and move on to another author once they've finished your book. And when you do have your second book ready, you'll have to start finding your audience all over again. It's much better to keep your audience by maintaining an ongoing relationship with them.

So, fiction authors—take a long view. Map out your second and third books before you finish your first. Figure out how to build your audience and keep them engaged over a long period.

A note about publishing economics

By the way, if you are a prolific writer, you may find you can slice your first manuscript into more than one book.

In today's world, it makes more sense (for most authors) to produce two 250-page novels than one 500-page work. If your readers enjoy your first book, then they will purchase your second. If competing books are priced at, say, $16.99 for 200 to 400-page books in your genre, why not give your audience two books for the price of two, rather than one book for the price of one? They will happily buy both. And you will happily enjoy a greater return on your investment.

Nonfiction needs your knowledge more than your writing skills.

If you are writing a nonfiction book, your most important attribute is your knowledge. It's not hard to purchase writing skills. That means if you find the writing task too challenging due to time availability, physical impairments, or lack of talent, don't worry. It's *your* knowledge and experience that need to be shared. So what's the solution? Hire a co-writer or ghostwriter or strong editor who will get your ideas into book form.

Some nonfiction authors—those who teach their material regularly—are surprised at the ease of creating a book from that material. One author was hesitant to write a book because he didn't think he could write well enough and didn't know how to start. I knew his work was important and needed to be shared, so I helped him outline the book's contents. His confidence rose as he realized he'd simply need to put on paper what he said to his clients and students over and over again.

If you are a subject matter expert, I advise you to take a similar approach. Ask, "What are the top eight or ten issues that come up all the time in my work with people?" Those eight or ten issues become the chapters of your nonfiction book. You simply explain each problem and offer appropriate solutions.

Subject matter experts: identify the top ten issues troubling your clients and make those the ten chapters of your book.

Or you can describe one or more processes you use to take clients from their starting point of problem or pain to the resolution of that problem or pain. Outline the steps you take them through; each one can be a chapter in your book. You've just described your process of problem resolution.

Another approach might be to capture your wisdom and insights based on years of experience in your field. Find *your* way to organize all the ideas into categories. Each category becomes a chapter in your book.

In nonfiction books like these examples, you might include case studies or stories of actual patients, students, or clients. Storytelling brings the concepts to life and ultimately makes your book more interesting to read.

Note: Be careful not to cross any lines of privacy so you don't open yourself to legal action. It's perfectly acceptable to change names and circumstances so your case studies remain confidential and individual identities are not exposed.

Writing your memoir

Memoirs feature all shapes and kinds. Literary memoirs such as *Angela's Ashes* by Frank McCourt or *A Year of Magical Thinking* by Joan Didion require exceptional writing skills. They incorporate writing techniques of fiction such as plot, dialogue, character development, story arc, descriptions that bring scenes to life, and so on. If you're not already a good writer, your goal to produce a literary memoir will demand your significant development as a writer.

On the other hand, if you want to provide a bit of your life history and stories so your family will know more about where they came from or what your life was like, you don't need to take it too seriously. Naturally you intend for your work to be readable and entertaining or informative, but it doesn't need to soar to great literary heights.

Note: A memoir is not the same as an autobiography. Autobiographies aim to be the complete factual record of a person's life, while memoirs can be a slice of one's experience or an arc of a life within a theme.

Most important, when writing your memoir, think about its purpose. If your memoir is for your family and friends, write what you want them to know. Do be conscious of others' feelings. When writing about people or events that you experienced, use phrases like "This is how I remember things ..." or "The way I experienced this event was ..." to forestall arguments about what really happened.

Be cautious about writing about other real people. Consider the hurt and anger your words might cause, even unintentionally. Find ways to tell your story without creating useless pain. And please don't write your book to hurt someone or to get revenge. That's a huge waste of creative effort.

Most memoirs written by unknown non-writers will have a slim audience of readers. If you want a larger audience, you'll need to have a reason to attract interest.

One woman I met had a moderately interesting life whose story would have been of interest only to family and friends. However, she wrote her story when she was in her late 70s because her cousin found dozens of letters and journals in their grandmother's attic. Those journals and letters provided the research material about the early days of the author's life. And the captivating element was the wrap-around story that her grandmother was a hoarder, which is why the journals and letters were still around, and the author herself was a psychiatrist who had treated hoarders! This book, if well-written, would have a marketing edge over similar ones because of the hoarder angle.

Chapter 6

Will you Choose Amateur or Professional Publishing?

Amateur (or informal) publishing refers to any form of self-publishing by someone not well versed in the publishing business. You can use CreateSpace or Lulu.com or Blurb. com or an online mega "self-publishing" corporation that invites unsuspecting authors into their high-pressure, low-quality publishing machines. But if you haven't educated yourself about the book publishing business, you must consider yourself an amateur.

If you have not educated yourself about the book publishing business, consider yourself an amateur.

Defining amateur (or informal) publishing

Take a moment to recognize deficiencies in your knowledge about publishing. Amateurs often *don't know what they don't know*, and that lack can lead to disappointment and wasted time, effort, and expense.

Most authors going the amateur route do so for financial reasons, but guess what! They often spend as much or more than they'd spend with a good contemporary publisher (see definition that follows), yet they end up with an amateur product because they bought the wrong services—often at inflated prices.

Be aware that the giant online "self-publishing" companies generally don't care much about the quality of the book you write, if a market for it exists, or how many books you might sell. If you give them a valid credit card, they will publish your book. They hard-sell their marketing services of questionable value at inflated prices, and they push authors to purchase large quantities of their own books at high prices.

Only a small percentage of self-published authors do enough of the necessary, intense work to become successful publishers. And generally they are the only successful self-published authors. It's possible, but you have to dedicate immense time and energy in becoming a publishing expert to self-publish sucessfully.

Defining professional hybrid/partner/ contemporary publishers

A new kind of publisher (Dudley Court Press, for example) has emerged in today's new world of publishing. They bridge the gap for authors who aren't likely to land a traditional publishing deal or who don't want that kind of arrangement, and/or who choose not to go the amateur, informal self-publishing route.

These contemporary publishers (sometimes called partner or hybrid) publishers operate with various business models, and the good ones are concerned with these four aspects of book publishing:

1. **Publishing quality books.** The best contemporary publishers have a selection process. They don't publish everything that comes in the door. They care about the writing and production quality because they're invested in the book's long-term potential for sales.

2. **Creating long-term publisher-author relationships.** The best contemporary publishers partner with authors throughout the process—planning, writing, design, marketing, and more. In the best of book publishing traditions, this relationship continues long after the book is printed.

3. **Producing to industry formats and standards.** Contemporary publishers can produce hardcover books, paperbacks, e-books, and audio books. They know how to include your book in industry databases and correctly format the book and its metadata used by search engines online. Also, authors retain the copyright to their work—a huge benefit.

4. **Ensuring book sales come from readers, not authors.** The best contemporary publishers—unlike many publishing service companies serving the self-publishing market—do NOT require the author to purchase copies of their book or pay near-retail prices for it. Contemporary publishers work

on behalf of and hand in hand with their authors to sell their books into the trade and special markets (bookstores, libraries, museum and gift stores, foreign markets, corporate markets, etc.).

Generally, in contemporary publishing models, authors pay fees for services and receive royalties on book sales. The long-term success of a contemporary publisher depends on those book sales, not on pumping a large number of authors through its system.

Look for a contemporary publisher that has the experience and knowledge to ensure a successful journey through the challenging world of publishing. Some innovative contemporary publishers have created new business models to take advantage of modern technologies and bring more high-quality books into the marketplace. For example, some contemporary publishers offer crowd-funding, auction markets for services, on-demand printing to avoid investment in inventory, author platform creation or managment, social media marketing, etc.

Defining traditional publishers

To attract their interest, traditional publishers generally require that you work with a literary agent, submit a book proposal, and show you have an established marketing platform (a ready-made customer base). They pay an advance against royalties for the rights to publish your book. As the author, you have little say about the manner of publishing, the timing of your book's release, or much else for the period the traditional publisher has the rights to publish your book. Although you pay no fees upfront, you are expected to participate in—and even contribute to—the costs of marketing your book.

As the world of book publishing continues to evolve rapidly, with new players, new technologies, new economic models and new standards emerging daily, every author will benefit from solid professional advice to ensure they are on the right track to publishing suceess.

Part Three

Phases of Writing and Publishing a Book

What You Don't Know about Writing and Publishing a Book: **The Six Phases**

Writing and publishing a book involves six major phases, some of which overlap. Every author should be knowledgeable about these aspects of the publishing journey to make sensible decisions along the way. The more you know as an author about each of these phases and your role in it, the more successful you will be. This section assumes you've found a publishing partner and have signed a publishing agreement.

The six phases are:

1. Manuscript preparation

2. Design (cover and interior layout)

3. Metadata Creation

4. Printing/Production (the manufacturing process)

5. Distribution

6. Marketing

Let's look at each phase in detail so you understand who and what is involved in each of them. As an author, it's important for you to know how to get the best help during each one, and how to assess the economics involved as you go along.

Chapter 7

Typing "The End" is Not the End: **Manuscript Preparation**

The "manuscript" is the name of your book's status before it's ready for design. This phase involves the author, any researchers or ghostwriters, all editors (developmental, content, and copy editors), and proofreaders. You're in charge as the writer, or you've engaged a ghostwriter to help complete the manuscript, and/or you're working with a publisher to shape the manuscript to meet the publisher's standards.

Research and writing stage

The process of creating the content (i.e., the research and writing of the book) can take weeks, months, or years. Every writer feels the same about this stage—that it's the hard part. While you're working on the writing, you look toward the day when you can type "The End" and celebrate all your hard work.

It is gratifying to reach that moment and deserves celebrating when you get there. However, it's also important for you, the author, to understand that this first part of the first phase—writing the content—is *not* the end. In fact, it's just the beginning. It signals the time to take off your Writer hat and put on your Author hat.

To be an author today means being the chief marketer of your book. And that starts in this first phase. Truthfully, it's best if marketing gets infused at the beginning of your authorship journey. The sooner you start being Chief Marketer of your book, the better.

Get clear...write directly...create relationships...

You do that by getting clear about *who* the audience is for your book, then writing directly to that audience, and creating relationships with people in that audience long before your book goes to press.

Editing stage

Once your manuscript is written, next comes editing it. You can save time and money by using inexpensive, or even free, editing software such as Hemingwayapp.com or Grammarly.com to do the first-round editing. These automated editing tools are invaluable for a writer, saving you money and time as you prepare your manuscript for review by a *real* editor.

First, understand the three levels of editing, which can overlap:

1. Developmental, also called structural or substantive editing;
2. Stylistic, also called content or line editing; and
3. Copy editing.

Developmental editing. Developmental editing focuses on the overall structure of the work. It ensures there's a logical flow to the chapters, that the story arc makes sense, and that the information is presented in an understandable, inviting manner. Because it takes place at the chapter level of organization, in a sense, you might say it *addresses the big picture.*

Content or line editing. Given the developmental editor works at the *chapter* level, the content or line editor works with the material on the *paragraph* level. The content editor ensures that sentences and paragraphs make sense and follow in logical sequences while looking for inconsistencies or redundancies in the text. He or she also points out muddy or unclear writing, the dreaded "purple prose" of amateur writers (highfalutin language with an excess of adjectives and adverbs), and places where readers will stumble or get lost.

A manuscript may go through several drafts with the content editor before it's ready for copy editing.

Copy editing. A copy editor works at the most detailed level, checking grammar, spelling, word usage, punctuation, and citations. He or she doesn't focus on content as much as the technical details of language usage. This step represents the first step in cleaning up the manuscript to prepare it for production.

Proofreading. This is the final step in preparing the manuscript for production. As a clean-up step, it ensures all the corrections recommended by the copy editor have been made.

Advice from a professional editor

I asked my good friend and editor, Barbara McNichol (www.BarbaraMcNichol.com), what advice she would give to a first-time author about the process of working with an editor. Here are highlights from our conversation:

Q. How can an editor help an author?

A. Smart authors know the value of a good editor to improve the clarity of their ideas and conciseness of the words they use. A good editor makes the author's prose more readable while preserving the person's intended voice.

Q. Can you advise authors on how to streamline their writing so the editing process goes more smoothly and costs less money?

A. Sure. Adopting these seven practices will make a huge difference in any manuscript:

1. Get rid of extraneous phrases (e.g., the fact of the matter is, there is and there are, is going to, is starting to, is designed to, etc.)

2. Find alternatives for wobbly words—vague words that don't add meaning (e.g., really, much, very, some, that).

3. Change long noun phrases into short verbs whenever feasible (e.g., "the examination of" becomes "examine"; "the judgment of" becomes "judge").

4. Limit the length of your sentences to about twenty words so readers won't get bogged down and lose your intended train of thought.

5. Pay attention to noun/verb agreements and pro- nouns, too. You hear people say "me and Michael went to lunch" but "me" is the wrong pronoun in this case. Know what's right. Apply the right gram- mar rules; it's important to your credibility!

6. Construct your sentences using active verbs, not passive (e.g., "The stranger created a scene" is ac- tive; "A scene was created by a stranger" is passive.) Why is this important? The action you want to con- vey moves forward more directly when you write in active construction. Look for the word "by," which clues you in to when passive construction is used.

7. For accuracy, know which word to use when. Pay special attention to confusing ones such as "com- plementary" versus "complimentary." Hint: the word "gift" and "complimentary" both have an "i" so when you're being complimentary, think of giv- ing away a gift. I call these "Word Trippers" and of- fer a word choice guide and subscription program to make it easy to learn the difference. (See www. wordtrippers.com)

Q. Why should someone invest in hiring a profes- sional editor?

A. Editors are trained to be patient and thorough. They go through an author's manuscript with a fine- toothed comb. That's rarely the kind of diligence provided by friends or even critique-group members. An author's work deserves the sharp, sustained focus of an experienced editor who will:

- Ensure wordiness doesn't turn your prose into a muddy bog that readers have to plod through.

- Move the prose forward with a feeling of lightness, not heaviness (e.g., using active voice, metaphors and similes, parallel structure, etc.).

- Embed styles and ensure formatting is consistent, thus making the book designer's job easier.

- Provide suggestions to improve the main title, subtitles, chapter titles, and subheads and add subheads where they enhance the reading.

- Correct grammar, spelling, and punctuation while making sure the "gremlins" don't get through—including any Word Trippers!

- Make the author's voice come through stronger and clearer than ever.

- Even add a touch of flair and artistry.

Q. Can you share an example of what an editor ought NOT to do?

A. Yes, and it's a personal story. Early in my career, I worked on a book for a Mississippi consultant whose branding reflected the Cajun culture. I diligently polished her chapters to perfection—smooth, slick, and business-like—but I went too far. Her charming Cajun expressions—what made her stand out among her peers and competitors—had disappeared. This taught me an important lesson. *A true editing partner strives to retain the author's voice.* I had crossed that fine line between improving the prose and rewriting it so much her voice didn't come through as she intended.

Q. Besides keeping the author's voice, what else is a primary goal in the editing process?

A. For nonfiction books especially, authors who are entrepreneurs write to support their business objectives. Their book forms the cornerstone of their company's message and direction. Keeping that objective in sight during the editing process guides the editor throughout the multiple reviews. Does the book accomplish what it sets out to do for the benefit of the readership and the author, too?

Q. What resources can you recommend for authors?

A. I recommend using the tools in Word as much as you can, including spellcheck (but don't rely on it) and its readability measure. For whacking wordiness in your prose, invest in Hemingway App (www.hemingwayapp.com). You would copy/paste a section of your writing into this app. It instantly notes where passive construction, long-windedness, and lack of clarity show up in your work. For knowing when to use the right word among confusing ones—accept vs. except, which vs. that—check out Word Trippers Tips (wordtrippers.com), a subscription program that includes an ebook of 390+ Word Trippers.

Barbara McNichol provides expert editing of books in the categories of business, spirituality, self-help, how-to, health, relationships, and memoirs. Over the past 23 years, she has placed *more than 340 books (and counting) on her editor's "trophy shelf." Barbara also helps authors and business people improve their writing through her ezine Add Power to Your Pen and her WordShop: "STRENGTHEN Everything You Write." Her comprehensive word choice guide **Word Trippers** is part of a 52-week subscription program called Word Trippers Tips. Full details at www.WordTrippers.com. Contact Barbara at 520-615-7910 or editor@barbaramcnichol.com. Please visit www. BarbaraMcNichol.com and connect on LinkedIn, Facebook, and Twitter.*

Manuscript submission requirements

Whether you find your publisher through a referral from your editor or a friend, or by searching online for a publisher or literary agent (try WritersMarket.com), when you contact a publisher, be sure to follow their submission requirements.

Most publishers will provide submission requirements for your manuscript at both the aquisition stage and for your completed manuscript. For example, you may be required to deliver a manuscript in a Word document, set up on 8.5 x 11 paper, portrait orientation, with one-inch margins, using Times New Roman, 12-point font, double-spaced, no formatting other than bold or italic, with any special formatting intentions spelled out in a separate area or document. You may be asked to submit a PDF file as an attachment, or to send a physical copy of your work.

You may be instructed to note all image insertions with brackets around the name of the image file and provide the images separately, with the image files labeled in a specified format. You may be told to include footnotes or to make all citations endnotes.

Sometimes you'll find that a publisher has word or page-count limits, usually to satisfy the specific marketing or design requirements. For example, your preferred publisher may want you to hold your novel to 300 pages because this is the targeted "sweet spot" that balances costs and revenues for this particular genre.

All this to say *pay attention to the manuscript submission requirements.* Your manuscript will be rejected by an aquisition team if it doesn't meet submission requirements. And once you've engaged with a publisher your manuscript will move more smoothly through the acquisition and production processes when you have followed instructions.

Once your manuscript is edited, copyedited, proofread and approved, it is ready to go to typesetting (also called layout.)

As an author, understand that, in a sense, your role as writer has ended. Next, you move fully into the role of marketer of your book, focusing first on its presentation, including the cover and interior design.

Chapter 8

A Book *is* Judged by Its Cover: **Design Phase**

Involving a book designer and/or interior layout artist, this phase includes creating the cover concept, final design, and preparing the cover files for printing. This happens along-side the design of the book's interior, layout of the interior's content, and preparation of the interior files for printing.

As a smart, exceptional author, you will want professionals to handle the design and layout of your book. Still, it's useful to understand key concepts and issues involved in your book's design. The more you know, the better decisions you can make and the more you can appreciate the value your professionals provide throughout the design process.

Cover design

Your book's cover design is such a critical element, it can mean sales or no sales, success or failure, reaching your audience or missing the mark. It's so important that I've asked my good friend and award-winning book designer Kathi Dunn of Dunn+Associates to share her insights. She can help you understand why your cover designer recommends certain choices over others. Here are highlights from our conversation:

Q. Let's start with the issue of fast and cheap book design, which is prevalent today. What's wrong with it?

A. Most authors would love to have their books designed and published "good, fast, and cheap." But you can't have all three of these.

The fast-and-cheap combo is popular, but it produces *substandard quality and cookie-cutter looks*—not a winning combination for selling a sizeable number of books or ensuring your book influences your brand positively.

Authors who go the fast-and-cheap route get a limited number of templates to choose from for their book covers. And if the company they work with is successful at selling their services to other price-sensitive authors, *even MORE books will look just like yours!* Plus, these "book production factories" have no time in the schedule or room in the budget to slow down and pay attention to quality or the author's brand.

The bottom line is when you pay dime-store publishing prices, you need to expect dime-store quality books.

Q. What does an experienced, professional designer bring to the table?

A. For a winning product, you need strong ideas, innovative design, and excellent technical execution. Veteran cover designers will ensure quality results and a cost-effective process based on their design experience. They act as your publisher's liaison who speaks the same language as the production people: prepress, printers, and manufacturers.

Q. Why is the cover design so important?

A. First of all, studies indicate that a potential buyer spends only eight seconds (or less) looking at your front cover and fifteen seconds looking at your back cover before making a buying decision. One literary agent told us her agency has a three-second rule—that is, the design must convey a clear pictorial message within three seconds of viewing it!

Second, bookstore distributors display only the book cover, not the books themselves. Therefore, a potential buyer has only the cover to go by when making a decision.

Third, seventy-five percent of booksellers say the cover is the most important element of the book. So if your book cover doesn't instantly hook a potential buyer's interest and then convey the right message about you, your chance to make a sale is gone.

By the way, if you're an author, speaker, or consultant who uses your book as an introductory product in a funnel of increasingly expensive products and services, when you lose the $19.95 book sale, you can also lose the thousands of dollars that customer might have spent on your audio programs, seminars, and coaching/consulting services.

Q. Besides attracting instant attention from readers and booksellers, what else can a great cover design do for an author?

A. A well-designed book can help you land a traditional publishing contract, secure fabulous reviews, establish your credibility as the expert, open all kinds of doors of opportunity, and generate a frenzy of book sales.

Q. How can first-time authors increase their chances of getting a great cover for their books?

A. The first step is to ensure that you and your publisher give the cover designer solid answers to these four questions to incorporate into the design:

1. Who is your target audience?
2. Who is your competition?
3. What sets you apart?
4. Where and how will you sell your product?

Your answers to these questions help the designer understand what your audience is expecting, what the norms are in your market and how to differentiate your book within those boundaries.

Q. What are some other elements of great cover design?

A. First, create a compelling, unique title and subtitle that relate to your defined market and offer concise benefits, features, and advantages.

Second, the title should be BIG! Stand six feet away, look at the cover, and ask, "What do I read first? What attracts my attention? What is my first impression of the nature of this product?" Also ask the same questions when looking at the cover image that's the size of a postage stamp onscreen.

Third, a good cover designer avoids clutter. The cover layout should be simple with appropriate type and imagery that lures the reader into purchasing the book.

More considerations are necessary, of course, including color choices, font selection, and integration of front, spine, and back cover. A professional book designer will tend to all of these concerns when developing your cover.

Q. What are the most common mistakes first-time authors make with their book covers?

A. Amateurs try to figure it out on their own, lean on friends' and family's opinions, or hire people who don't know the intricacies of the industry. They end up with books that don't appeal to their buying audience and/or don't meet industry standards for distribution.

Q. When should authors start thinking about the cover design for their books?

A. The front cover should be created as soon as the book's title is solid. Because the front cover is the book's most important marketing piece, professional publishers have the front cover design produced before the manuscript is finished. Getting it done early not only brings the book to reality but also provides early marketing opportunities to create a buzz—and even pre-sales. Simply posting the front cover mock-up above the author's work space propels him or her to the finish line.

The spine and back cover are designed last, right before heading to press or final production. Your publisher often waits until several reviews and endorsements are submitted so they can be woven into the sales copy.

The spine cannot be designed until there is a firm page count since that drives the dimension of the spine. By the way, amateur authors don't often understand the importance of the spine in the retail environment. Books sold in brick-and-mortar stores are usually displayed spine out. A seasoned cover designer will treat the spine as a mini-front cover, knowing it must jump off the shelf into the bookstore browser's hands compared with competing titles.

It takes time and thought to create a marketable spine, small as it seems.

Dunn+Associates helps serious authors, fast-track speakers, and information marketers build business empires with best-selling book covers, powerful promotional tools, and strategic brand design. Its designers have created hundreds of award-winning book covers for numerous best-sellers. Clients have included leading authors and speakers such as Tony Robbins, Mark Victor Hansen, Jack Canfield, Ken Blanchard, John Edward, and Deepak Chopra as well as major publishers, including HarperCollins, Simon and Schuster, Prentice-Hall, and Hay House. Visit www.dunn-design.com or call 715-634-4857.

Interior design and layout

First-time authors generally haven't given much thought to the interior design of their book. One way to become educated about quality in interior design is to look at several professionally published books in your genre. Note these details:

- Fonts used
- Heading and footer styles
- Treatment of chapter titles
- Initial paragraph design
- Decorative elements
- Treatment of images and captions
- Treatment of tables, lists, and figures
- Design of call-outs (text that's set off and not included directly in the main text)

These and other elements impact the design decisions a good interior book designer will consider when laying out your book. Amateur authors overlook the importance of good design. Professional publishers invest in creating appropriately designed books to meet market expectations and the author's goals.

Recently I interviewed Maggie Urgo, a friend and professional book designer who has decades of experience. I asked her to share details about how professional interior book designers work so first-time authors could gain an appreciation of the process.

Q. Why is the *interior* design of a book important?

A. While covers represent and concentrate on the content of the book, interiors actually *are* the book. They must be legible and easy to follow so they keep the reader's attention from start to finish.

Many important but often subtle industry standards such as fonts, headers, layout, and more differentiate a professionally designed book from one that is not.

Q. Let's talk about fonts. Many amateur authors go overboard with fonts, thinking that variety is the spice, I guess. What advice can you give first-time authors about the wise use of fonts?

A. Professional designers often restrict their fonts in any given project to one serif font (letters with "feet") and one sans serif font (no "feet"). We use various weights (bold, italics, etc.) of those fonts for variety, but we avoid a potpourri of fonts used only for decoration.

In book interiors, font use should help the reader move easily through the text, reflecting the author's intentions for the flow, emphasis, feel, and organization of the materials.

Q. What are "running heads" and "running feet"?

A. Those are industry terms for what are also called headers and footers. They should be so subtle you barely notice them, but they play an important role in orienting the reader as to where they are in a book.

Headers and/or footers contain the page numbers and chapter titles or section titles and sometimes subhead information. They should be separate enough from the body text so they don't look like part of the story, but close enough so they aren't floating out in space.

These two important best practices will immediately distinguish a professionally designed book from an amateur book:

1. Headers and footers should not appear on the title page.

2. Headers, footers, and page numbers should not appear on blank pages. (Blank pages count in the numbering but don't show the number itself.)

Q. What are "front matter" and "end matter"?

A. Front matter refers to everything that goes in the beginning of a book before the main body of the book, including endorsements, copyright page, half-title, full title, epigraph, dedication, table of contents, list of illustrations, (sometimes) acknowledgements, and so on. The treatment of front matter distinguishes professionally designed books from amateur books. Each type of front matter has a fairly standard design treatment in the industry and looks different from the main part of the book. For example, copyright pages are almost always on the reverse side of the title page and are set in very small type.

Unsurprisingly, end matter (or back matter) refers to the parts of the book at the end, including endnotes, appendices, (sometimes) acknowledgments, and About the Author materials. Much of this text can be smaller than the main body text, especially the endnotes.

Q. Let's turn to the relationship between the cover and the interior design. What should a first-time author know?

A. The title page and the chapter titles are the showy design elements of the interior. One of my personal pet peeves is when the title page and the chapter titles fail to blend with the cover. When they don't, you know that sufficient attention hasn't been paid to the project. Whatever tone the cover establishes should carry over into the interior.

Q. What's your advice to first-time authors about the treatment of images and captions?

A. Be prepared to work with your publisher early on in the process when your book involves images. Paper choice and the quality, resolution, and size of your images need to be considered to ensure satisfactory results. Your publisher should have the designer vet the images. If publisher reps aren't sure you'll be able to get good reproduction, they may request a test image proof from the printer— that is, a printed sample of the images only. That way you can see what quality you will get.

In certain instances, image quality may not be as important as content. For example, if you've written a memoir and have only one photo of yourself as a child at age ten in a whole chapter written about that stage of your life, you may have no choice. Even professional book designers sometimes use low quality images if they are clearly important to the story. The readers will understand. It's also possible a designer can improve the quality of the image using various restoration tools available.

Q. What about the treatment of tables, charts, and similar elements?

A. Tables and lists, charts and graphs can add richness and a lot of information to certain types of books. Consider if your chart, graph, table, or fill-in-the blanks question actually needs to be in a particular place in the text. Perhaps you can write your book so they can be placed near where they should be.

Here's an example. See the difference between a manuscript that says:

Write your 5 personal goals on the 5 blank lines provided below:

_____

_____

_____

_____

_____

And a manuscript that says:

Write your 5 personal goals on the 5 blank lines provided in the Personal Goals box, then continue reading.

[designer, please create a box with 5 blank lines, title it "Personal Goals" and place near this text]

Why is this difference important? And why is the second way considerably better? Suppose this chunk of text ends up at the bottom of a page and only four of the lines will fit. Then the stray fifth line ends up on the top of the next page. Or suppose you have a chart that should be four inches tall but the designer has only three inches of room left on that page. Either the designer leaves a big blank hole at the bottom of the page and moves the chart to the next page or shrinks it to fit, and it becomes illegible.

The principle is this: any charts, photos, tables, graphs, or other elements such as call-outs you want to include should be referenced in the text in a way that leaves flexibility in their positioning within the text.

Your publisher and book designer will appreciate it if you create your manuscript with this in mind.

Q. What about "air" and "white space"?

A. In design terms, "air" means white space—that is, space where nothing is there. A design with page after page of dense small type with no subheads, no call-outs, small margins, and short paragraph indents becomes crowded and deadly boring. These elements also work against the reader's enjoyment and continued attention. The same manuscript can be used to create books with different page counts, qualitatively more or less expensive, depending on how "airy" the design is.

Unless your book is a "must read" (which is true for some scientific and technical works), then be aware of the need for air, even if it means more pages and a somewhat more expensive product. This particularly applies to novels where there may be few chapters and no subheads, images, charts, or other design elements. A designer has several ways to introduce "air" into the design: wide margins, deep paragraph indents, call-outs, charts, and photos.

Q. Anything else that first-time authors should know?

A. Yes, margins! The inside margin must be large enough that a reader doesn't have to "break the back" of a book to see all the type on the page. Also, realize that a professionally designed book is not centered on the page but pushed to the right on the right-hand page (recto) and to the left on the left-hand page (verso) to accommodate a wider interior margin (known as the "gutter").

Finally, Word is a great program for writing your manuscript. It is *not* used for professional book layout.

Maggie Urgo began her career as an art director for several New York ad agencies, notably DDB and Young and Rubicam. She has been a book designer for over 19 years and a graphic designer for longer than that. She supervised the design department at a highly respected Chicago publishing company for 10 years. She also worked as a designer at a cutting-edge textbook publishing company in Chicago and did a stint as a production manager and occasional designer for Smith, Badovfsky & Raffel, an award-winning boutique ad agency in Chicago.

She has won awards from The Art Directors Club of New York, Print Magazine, the American Institute of Graphic Arts and the Chicago book clinic, among others.

Chapter 9

Unseen and Unknown: **Metadata, Manufacturing, Distribution**

Metadata

Metadata refers to the information that's created or required about your book: industry identifiers as the ISBN, bar code, LCCN and PCIP data block; descriptive information such as categories (BISAC, Amazon, Kindle), the book's title and subtitle, its description and keywords; and more. Your publishing partner should carefully create and manage data elements to ensure your book can be found by potential booksellers and readers. Several are described here.

ISBN. The ISBN is the International Standard Book Number, a 13-digit (since 2007) number that uniquely identifies both the publisher and the edition of a book. In the United States, R. R. Bowker (bowker.com) is the ISBN agency that sells and maintains the official database of ISBN records for books published by U.S. publishers.

Remember:

- An ISBN is unique to the specific edition of a specific book.

- The ISBN has imbedded in it a reference to the publisher of record. The purchaser of the ISBN from Bowker is identified as the publisher of the book associated with the ISBN.

- Your book does not need an ISBN if it won't to be sold commercially through bookstores, other retailers, or to libraries.

- Your book does not need an ISBN if it will be sold **only** on Amazon, as a print book and/or as a Kindle ebook, because Amazon will assign its own unique ASIN to your product. (ASIN means Amazon Standard Identification Number.)

Bar code. The bar code is the graphic with the vertical lines used for scanning purposes. It often, but not always, includes price information as well as the book's edition identifier. The bar code can be generated by any number of software programs or online providers once the correct information is provided.

LCCN. An LCCN is the Library of Congress Control Number assigned to the bibliographic record created by the Library of Congress or another library for a given book. It is unique to each book record. An LCCN must be requested through the Library of Congress.

PCIP or CIP. A PCIP (publisher's cataloging-in-publication) data block is a bibliographic record prepared according to Library of Congress specifications. It's included on the copyright page to facilitate book processing for libraries and book dealers. If the Library of Congress creates the record, it's called a CIP. The format for CIP (and PCIP) blocks was changed in September, 2015.

NOTE: If you want your book to be considered by libraries for their collections, it's a good idea for your book to display both the LCCN and PCIP block in addition to the ISBN and bar code.

Categories. Another aspect of your book's metadata concerns the categories your publisher assigns to it for bookstore, library, and Amazon categorization purposes. It's important that your book be shelved (either physically or in terms of search criteria) in the most appropriate locations where people would be looking for a book like yours. There's an art to choosing appropriate categories.

The Book Industry Study Group (BISG) is responsible for creating the BISAC category list, which is the dominant category list in the industry. BISAC (Book Industry Standards and Communications) categories change frequently. In fact, the 2016 list featured about 500 changes.

Amazon and Kindle each have their own category lists, and they are not the same as either BISAC or each other's list.

A wise publisher uses categories strategically, especially on Amazon and Kindle, to help your book be discovered more easily. For example, placing it in an appropriate but lightly populated category can cause your book to rise to the top in its category more easily, thus possibly earning greater distinction and recognition.

Using category selection properly and strategically helps improve your book's chances of being discovered. Poor or ineffective use of categories practically guarantees your book will be among the millions no one ever finds.

Title and subtitle. The decision about your book's title and subtitle should not center on cute, clever, or (worse) mysterious. Fiction titles are, of course, a different animal than nonfiction titles. For nonfiction, use the title to express what's in the book. If you can't convey the book's message in the title, then at least do it in the subtitle. Otherwise, your audience may never find your book. Remember, the title and cover design of your book should work together to convey the content of your book and never be at odds with each other.

Description. How you describe your book becomes a marketing tool. Your publisher will include a well-written description when your book is registered on R. R. Bowker, when it's submitted to Amazon and other retailers, when creating a sell sheet for your book, and in many, many other places. Your publisher should ensure your description works to market your book by including keywords and clear, appealing benefits to the reader. The task of writing a compelling book description should not be taken lightly. To be effective, it should be a solid piece of sales copy written by a professional and used consistently across all formats and sales outlets.

Keywords, keyword search terms. Though these are *last* on this list of metadata elements, keywords are *first* on the list of elements to be created to support publishing and marketing your book. In today's world, having strong keywords and longer search terms in your title, subtitle, and description have become essential to gaining recognition on Google. More generic keywords work better on Amazon. Strategic use of keywords is vital to discoverability.

With all the elements noted here—title, subtitle, description, keywords, etc.—ensure they're created with discoverability and merchandising in mind.

Manufacturing

Books can be printed on demand or in print runs. The term "on demand" (POD, print-on-demand) refers to the idea of manufacturing the book only when it's ordered, thus avoiding costs of large print runs with associated inventory handling and storage costs. On-demand printing is always digital and generally involves printing one to a few hundred copies. For paperbacks, this method is fast and readily available.

By comparison, print runs mean you create inventory that's kept on hand to meet orders. Print runs can be done on digital printers or offset printers. Digital printing is often used for runs up to about 1,000 copies; offset printing becomes price competitive at runs of about 1,500 and up. Of course, many details affect the choice of printing technology, including trim size, binding, paper choice, unit quantity, color versus black and white, time schedule, etc.

Print books can be soft cover (paperback) or hardcover (case bound) with various kinds of binding. Perfect bound is the most common type of paperback binding today. Today, e-book and audio book formats are additional production options for your book.

Clearly, how much money you have available to invest will affect how your book is manufactured, which dictates how much profit your book can make.

Distribution

Distribution refers to the ways in which the book becomes accessible to the ultimate purchaser. Usually to get books into retail bookstores, libraries, and specialty stores, a publisher works with distributors and/or wholesalers. Distributors represent many publishers and hundreds, if not thousands, of titles. Usually the distributor will hold inventory and fulfill orders, but various arrangements are possible. Sales into bookstores are usually returnable. Note: the returns (unsold books) from bookstores are a real and significant cost to publishers.

Amateur publishers are generally unschooled in many important aspects of the book publishing process. To ensure your book has a chance for sales success, seek a strong professional publishing partner to handle all these phases.

Chapter 10

Start Today
and Never Stop:
Marketing

As emphasized in Chapter 2, if you intend to write a book, you'll need to market it as well—and incessantly.

The best marketing is built into your book: its title, subtitle, cover design, description, category selection, and other metadata elements. Your best marketing starts now—and never ends.

> *The best marketing is built into your book. And*
> *the best marketing starts now—and never ends.*

Marketing begins with the book concept and should be considered a parallel phase to all the other phases, and one that never stops. No book can make its way to readers without readers knowing about it. Every author needs to think about how to reach his or her audience long before the book is finished.

You will find 72 million search results on Google when you type in "book marketing ideas" so there's no shortage of ideas. The key to book marketing success is twofold: choose a few ideas and put them into action. Then repeat. And repeat. And repeat.

Five first steps to take NOW to market your book

Every author can take these five simple first steps that begin to build the necessary marketing foundation or platform:

1. **Purchase appropriate website domains**. The cost of a URL is minimal and good URLs will help people find you and your book. For starters, get www.your name.com or a simple variation that won't be confusing. Also purchase the domain name that's relevant to your book title as soon as you have chosen the title. NOTE: You won't necessarily create websites for all the domain names you choose; you can point many URLs to your main website. You, not your publisher or marketing partner, should own all the URLs related to your book and brand. These are business assets and therefore should be considered and managed as such.

2. **Add marketing elements to your email signature**. At the very least, add "Author of the forthcoming book, *Title of Your Book*." You can add: "to be released spring, 20__ by [name-of-your-publisher]." Even include a one to eight-word description of your book or genre. Everyone who reads an email from you will know your book is on its way.

3. **Establish your email list.** Sign up for a free Mailchimp account or use any other recognized system so you can build this key asset. Cultivate the belief that your email list is an asset while social media followers and friends are ephemeral. Remember to ASK PERMISSION to email people. This has become more and more important, so don't ignore this essential element of good marketing. Begin regular habits of communicating with your list to further your relationships. Do NOT spam and do NOT buy names. Instead, build your list methodically and authentically. A small list of committed followers is far more valuable than a huge list of uninterested—and too often fake—names. If you spam, you're likely to be blacklisted, and besides, it's just not nice.

4. **Create a professional-looking website.** If you're aiming for any sort of commercial recognition and success as an author or expert, you'll need a website. Be sure it's mobile optimized, is secure (with an https: prefix, not http:) and is optimized for search engines. Hire a good web development firm that knows design, copy writing, and digital marketing for this. Your website is an important business asset; invest in quality.

5. **Create and use a blog to feed the search engines.** Think of your blog as the feeding trough for search engine robots or crawlers. Feed the "bots" regularly and consistently with strong content that is search-engine optimized (but not overly

so) and related to you and your topic. Use images and videos in your blog posts, properly labeled and optimized. This regular diet provided to the bots, spiders, and crawlers is the most important thing you can do to help your book get found on the Internet, i.e., to show up in the top search results when someone searches for you or your topic. The longer you have been feeding the bots, crawlers, and spiders, the more credibility you have with them—as long as the "food" is good. That's why it's critical to have more than only a tech person build a website for you. Be sure to engage a digital marketing professional (and your granddaughter who "loves Snapchat" doesn't qualify!). Starting now is wise; six months from now, you'll be six months ahead of where you would be if you had waited.

A bonus idea

Here's a bonus idea: Once your book cover is done, create business cards, bookmarks, and/or postcards to promote you and your book. Put your book cover on one side and your information on the other—a great way to communicate and share your book's availability.

Think ahead to how to use postcards or bookmarks for various purposes. Have the front printed in a large quantity, in color, four-up, but don't cut them. Then use those sheets in small quantities for specific uses (e.g., postcard mailers, special offers, book-signing announcements, etc.). You can print information on the back side in black and white before cutting.

You've got millions of book marketing ideas just waiting for you on the Internet. The essential ingredient only *you* can provide is action.

Four more marketing actions

After beginning to create your author platform with those first five steps, here are a few more ideas that can provide significant payoff:

1. **Ask for reviews.** Reviews on Amazon, Goodreads, and other places become the social proof that helps sell your book. Seek out reviewers diligently. Don't stop until you have 25 four- or five-star reviews on Amazon. Then continue asking until you reach 100.

2. **Market to your target audience via social media.** Start with one or two platforms (e.g., Facebook, Twitter, LinkedIn, Pinterest, Instagram) and learn to use them to your best advantage. Don't waste idea time on social media; use it to market your book. Learn how to do that effectively or hire an experienced person to help you.

3. **Identify and reach out to local media.** Wherever you live, there are readers for you. You'll find them through your local media—print, radio, and TV. Do the research to find the right journalists, program hosts, and producers—and keep your database up to date. Remember this important point: *The news is NEVER that you published a book.* Instead, find a hook that serves the interests of the audience that the journalist/producer/talk show host cares about.

4. **Use personal and professional affiliations**. Note all the institutions and organizations of which you are a member or have an affiliation. Think about how you can serve those audiences. Can you offer to speak on your topic? Can you write an article for their newsletters? Would it be sensible to place an ad in their newsletter?

No matter what aspect of book marketing you engage in, orient your thinking away from selling your book and toward solving problems for people in your audience. You should clearly specify the benefits to the reader of buying and reading your book as well as state the problem(s) your book solves. You should be able to explain the topic your book covers and why a reader should care. When you can do those things, then look for angles that relate to those benefits, those problems for which you have a solution. The solutions and benefits are what interest the audience and thus the media.

_____

The publicity you attract by using interesting hooks and angles will sell your book.

_____

Remember, the existence of your book is NOT the angle that will get the publicity you want. But the publicity you attract by using interesting hooks and angles will sell your book. Invest in quality marketing to help you enjoy the most return on your investment.

Chapter 11

Conclusion:
Your Next Step

Make a decision.

That's the first next step. Decide to answer the call to write a book or decide that the time is not right and move on to other things with a clear head.

Be honest about your goals.

Take the time to get very clear about why you are writing your book and what the emotional payoff will be for you when it is done. Write down the reasons. Write down the outcome. Be clear about the role this book-writing and the final product, your book, will have in your life.

Be honest about your investment/budget.

Be aware of the zeitgeist that says publishing a book is free. It's not.

Write down how much time and money you intend to invest in this book project. Be clear about what you need help with, and investigate the costs.

Consider how you make other purchasing decisions, especially in areas where you lack knowledge. Do you get professional help with taxes? Do you hire someone to help with interior design for your home? Golf or art lessons? Do you pay for business advice?

When it comes to your book project, do you know what you don't know, and do you know how that can hurt you?

If you're trying to justify the expense, consider what you spend in a year on hobbies or, if this will be a book related to your business, on other marketing activities for your business.

Consider what the long-term rewards might be once your book is done. Keep in mind book sales or royalties, new clients, larger audiences, more media exposure, etc. Or perhaps pride of authorship and satisfaction when you see your book on your bookshelf.

Ideas to get started

Today…Do something to get things moving.

Make writing dates with yourself. Put them on your calendar.

Create a mock-up cover of your book and put it where you can see it every day for inspiration and motivation.

Set a deadline for when you want to hold your book in your hands.

Make a list of the major tasks you need to accomplish to reach that deadline.

Map out your timeline.

And, if professional publishing is your preferred route, consider working with a contemporary publisher such as Dudley Court Press. We offer a complimentary, no obligation, 30-minute Introductory Call to help you determine how best to proceed with your book project. It's an easy way to move forward.

Visit our Get Started page now—and get started!
https://www.DudleyCourtPress.com/GetStarted2

Acknowledgements

Thank you to Bob Barnhill, Katie Goodwin, and Jason and Stacey Ansley for reading this book in its early stages; to Barbara McNichol for your fine editing hand; to Maggie Urgo for your delightful interior design and to Kathi Dunn and Hobie Hobart for your brilliant cover design and helpful support throughout.

Thank you also to all the DCP Book Reviewers who have been kind enough to purchase, read and review this book on Amazon and other online sites. I appreciate your support!

About the Author

Gail Woodard is the author of four books and CEO of Dudley Court Press. A frequent speaker and presenter at industry conferences, Gail has an MBA from Yale University and worked for many years as a consultant and executive in the real estate and banking industries. She has also been a visiting instructor at several universities.

Woodard has resided in France, Mexico, Ecuador, Nicaragua, and Brazil and traveled to 22 other countries. Currently, she lives contentedly in Sonoita, Arizona, where she's learning to love the javelinas, or at least coexist with them.

Connect with Gail at www.DudleyCourtPress.com or on Facebook, Twitter or LinkedIn.

DUDLEY COURT PRESS
Sonoita, Arizona

Dudley Court Press is a trusted contemporary publisher dedicated to helping exceptional authors bring meaningful books to the world. Our partnerships with our clients begin with a strategy session and continue long after a book is published. Publishing programs cover editing, design, printing/manufacturing, distribution for paperback, hardcover, ebook and audiobooks and ongoing marketing opportunities for foreign rights and library sales, book signings at prestigious events, competitions, targeted advertising and promotional events. Learn more at www.DudletCourtPess. com.

What's a Strategy Session?

A Strategy Session is a three- to four-hour conversation with Dudley Court Publisher Gail Woodard by phone or Skype.

A Strategy Session helps fit publishing dreams or plans into an overall career or life plan, whether you're writing fiction or nonfiction, for personal or commercial purposes. Strategy Session clients uniformly express gratitude for the wealth of knowledge they receive and the clarity they gain about their publishing paths.

Your Strategy Session helps you uncover:

- what you hope to accomplish,
- where you are in the book project process,
- who the intended audience of your book is,
- your production options and preferences,
- your expectations for marketing, distribution, and sales, and
- your budget.

During a Strategy Session, you'll gain clarity about the book contents, the target audience, the writing process, the required resources, the likely timetable, your publishing choices, and your book's marketing requirements. After a Strategy Session, you can follow your new roadmap alone or, if both parties agree, with Dudley Court Press as your publishing partner. Interested? Start here: www.DudleyCourtPress.com/GetStarted2

DCP Book Reviewer Panel

If you love reading books as much as I do, then join our Reviewer Panel. We want YOU in our community!

Be Heard, Get Rewarded

Joining the reviewer community is always free and you'll get these exclusive benefits:

- Free books and special discount codes
- Early access to promotions and new releases of meaningful books
- Special online events where you can connect with authors
- Invitations you won't find anywhere else

DCP's Book Reviewer Panel is a place for you to discover interesting new books and share your thoughts. Leaving an honest review online can help authors improve their message and get found by other readers. (We know that Amazon's automated system looks at the number and quality of reviews when selecting the books to display in response to customers' searches, so reviews improve a book's "discoverability.")

Don't worry if you haven't reviewed books before; no special skills are required. We can show you how to write a good review and how to post it online.

Join Now

Ready for interesting new books, exciting benefits and the chance to help authors get found? Join the DCP Book Reviewer Panel today! You can sign up here: www.DudleyCourtPress.com/Reviewer-Panel

Index

Enjoy these other meaningful books from Dudley Court Press

Yoga for Pain Relief: A new approach to an ancient practice. *Lee Albert, NMT.*

For anyone who suffers from painful muscular conditions on or off the mat. This book shows readers how to identify the specific muscle imbalance that cause their pain and provides easy-to-follow instructions to create a safe yoga practice to rebalance the body.

ISBN: 9781940013329   2017   160 pages $29.95

Softening the Grief: What to say and do to comfort a bereaved mother. *Joan E. Markwell with Janie Fields, Patricia Hollingsworth and Suzie McDonald.*

A companion for grieving mothers and a resource for people who care but are afraid they will say the wrong thing. Written by four bereaved mothers, this book educates friends and family. Includes 25 hurtful things people say and offers better ways to communicate compassion and support.

ISBN: 9781940013411   2017   170 pages $14.99

B-17 Flying Fortress Restoration: The story of a WWII bomber's return to glory in honor of the veterans of the Mighty Eighth Air Force. *Jerome McLaughlin*

Weaves lively narrative and first-person accounts to capture the restoration of the WWII-vintage Boeing B-17 bomber now housed in the Combat Gallery at the National Museum of the Mighty Eighth Air Force in Pooler, GA. Includes hundreds of pictures, historical vignettes and the full story from the airplane's arrival in pieces on the back of several tractor-trailers, through years of painstaking restoration of its aluminum skin, operating systems, armament and even its nose art.

ISBN: 9781940013251   2016   304 pages $24.95

Mountain Majesty: The history of CODEP Haiti where sustainable agricultural development works, Volumes 1 & 2. *John Winings.*

Tells the inspiring story that began in 1989 when a U.S. volunteer recognized that the solution to poverty in Haiti's Cormier Valley lay in addressing the entire watershed not just a few local gardens. During its 25-year history, CODEP Haiti has championed reforestation and erosion control, found creative solutions to engage the local population and converted a church-subsidized development program into a self-sustaining, locally managed enterprise.

Vol 1 ISBN: 9781940013213   2015   206 pages $16.99
Vol 2 ISBN: 9781940013336   2016   206 pages $18.99

On My Watch: leadership, innovation, & personal resilience. *Martha Johnson*

When a scandal emerged over a GSA training conference in Las Vegas, Martha Johnson, Administrator of the General Services Administration for President Obama, was compelled to resign. Despite the uproar of the moment, Johnson asserts that the real story of GSA was the extraordinary innovation underway at the agency. *On My Watch* illuminates her tenure at GSA and her leadership strategies of innovation, interruption, transparency and design in the face of seemingly intractable problems.

ISBN: 9781940013015   2013   181 pages $19.95

Zero to a Billion: 61 rules entrepreneurs need to know to grow a government contracting business. *David Kriegman*

An insightful, practical, how-to guide for entrepreneurs who want to build a successful government contracting business. The author draws on his thirty years of experience to illustrate the essential lessons of strategy, business development, cultural issues and operations with real-world examples and actionable ideas. Highly recommended for new and mid-career managers as well as seasoned executives.

ISBN: 9781940013046   2013   196 pages $21.95

DCP books are available online and through booksellers everywhere.

For more information about these and other books published by Dudley Court Press, please visit our online bookstore at www.DudleyCourtPress.com/Books